INVITATIONS

of JESUS

Trevor Hudson

UPPER
ROOM BOOKS®
NASHVILLE

The Upper Room® website http://www.upperroom.org

UPPER ROOM®, UPPER ROOM BOOKS®, and design logos are trademarks owned by The Upper Room®, A Ministry of GBOD®, Nashville, Tennessee. All rights reserved.

Scripture quotations are from the New Revised Standard Version Bible, copyright 1989 National Council of the Churches of Christ in the United States of America. Used by permission. All rights reserved.

Instructions for *lectio divina* adapted from "Praying the Scriptures" by Beth Richardson for *Alive Now*. Used by permission.

Cover and interior design: Marc Whitaker / www.mtwdesign.net

Printed in the United States of America

CONTENTS

How to Use This Book

As you read each week's meditation, you will be prompted to wonder about how the ideas in the book intersect with your own life. These *Wonderings* are invitations to stimulate your imagination and draw you into prayer; they are invitations from God. How will you respond to these invitations? Reflect on the questions and write your answers in a journal. Reflecting and journaling in this way will take you deeper into each invitation.

The weekly readings and *Wonderings* will facilitate personal reflection on your interests, preferences, and talents. These questions and journaling will require no more than ten to fifteen minutes daily.

If you choose to use this book in a small-group setting, you will meet weekly with others to reflect on the lesson's readings and *Wonderings*. The Leader's Guide for leading a small group is found at the back of the book. Bring this book, your Bible, and a journal with you to each weekly meeting.

Week One

INVITATION
TO
LIFE AT
ITS BEST

"I came that they may have life,

and have it abundantly."

– JOHN 10:10

The other day I came across an unopened invitation. It was an invitation to the wedding reception of a couple I married almost a year ago. They gave it to me after a premarital counseling session. I placed it on my desk and forgot about it. When I eventually came across the invitation hidden under a pile of papers and opened it, my heart sank. The young couple had wanted my wife, Debbie, and me to celebrate with them and their friends after the wedding ceremony. By overlooking their generous invitation, I had missed out on experiencing an event that was no doubt very special.

As I began to write on the invitations of Jesus, I immediately remembered that unopened invitation. In life, we can miss out on so much. It may be sharing a meal, celebrating a birthday, witnessing a baptism, or, like it was for me, celebrating the covenant of a new marriage. Our sadness deepens with the knowledge that, when we realize we have not responded to an invitation, we cannot turn back the clock. Our loss is forever.

For many years now the invitations of Jesus have gripped my imagination because they lead us into the abundant life Jesus promises to those who respond to him. "I came," Jesus tells us, "that they may have life, and have it abundantly" (John 10:10). When people ask me why I take Jesus' invitations so seriously, this sentence always springs to mind. I accept invitations not because they satisfy my every need, remove all my problems, or make me feel good; I accept them because I am convinced that through them, we discover how life can be most truly and fully lived.

THE NEW WAY OF LIFE JESUS OFFERS

This conviction about the good news Jesus brings gradually wove itself into the fabric of my believing. But that was not always the case. In the early years of my faith pilgrimage, I restricted the primary purpose for God coming in Christ to the forgiveness of sins. I understood that to be the main gospel invitation. In everyday language, I would put it like this: Come to Jesus, get your sins forgiven, and go to heaven. While that message contains a wonderful truth, somehow it is not true enough. Let me explain.

As I have studied the invitations of Jesus in the Gospels and mulled over the insights of significant mentors, my understanding of the good news has grown considerably from what I first understood it to be. I have come to see that the central issue of the gospel of Jesus involves the gracious opportunity to become a new kind of person and to enter into a new way of life. Available to anyone who responds wholeheartedly to the invitations of Jesus, his gospel embraces both the forgiveness of our sins and the recovery of abundant life.

Before we go further, notice the striking relevance of this good news to our lives today. In spite of the flood of techniques for self-fulfillment and personal contentment, our world is increasingly full of despair, suicide, addiction, emptiness, and a tragic inability to get along with those we want to love. To put it bluntly, we appear to have little idea about how to live. Jesus' invitations possess an enduring relevance: they invite us—in the same way they invited the first disciples—into life at its very best.

RSVP

How do we respond to the invitations of Jesus? First of all, like all invitations, we need to open them. I remember the first time I went through all the recorded words of Jesus, paying particular attention to each specific invitation. While I refer to only five of them in this book, many more appear throughout the Gospels. Each one reminds us that God does not force the gospel upon us; rather, God seeks our freely given and thoughtful responses. There are three phases of response to the invitations of Jesus:

1. *Open.* First, we need to recognize and understand what Jesus' invitations actually are. We agree to open the invitation and see what it is—that is, read the scripture and receive the invitation.
2. *Explore.* Second, we explore the invitations as fully and as carefully as we can. What do they tell us about the God we worship? How do they describe for us the life Christ offers us? How do they relate to our everyday lives and

relationships? Is there anything that we are being asked to do? Sometimes answering these questions take time. What Jesus invites us to is not always immediately clear. It may take a few days, weeks, or even months to understand what is involved. Let us not be deterred. Not only can we help each other through this time of exploration and waiting, but also Jesus has promised that his Spirit will be our teacher and guide.

3. *Respond.* We eventually reach a time when we feel prepared to respond to Jesus' invitations. Hopefully we will say yes! The challenge of faith is to stake our lives on these invitations.

In New Testament Greek, the word for faith is a verb. Faith involves not only believing certain truths but also taking action. Faith in Jesus means opening his invitations, exploring them as thoroughly as we can, and then responding to them in our everyday lives. Unless we move through this process toward offering a response, we will not experience the fullness of life that the gospel promises.

Let me offer my simple testimony. Over the years I have learned that those who respond to Jesus' invitations receive a gracious gift. Jesus, through the power of his Spirit, emerges from the pages of the Gospels, steps into our lives, and becomes an empowering presence. Amazingly, we discover how Jesus can be our living friend and companion as he was for those who accepted his invitations long ago. As we fall into step with him and with the community of other believers, Jesus shows us the way to live and provides us the strength to follow him. That's when we begin to discover life at its best.

Over eighteen centuries ago, Saint Irenaeus penned this provocative sentence: "The glory of God is a human being who is fully alive." Whatever else these words may mean, his insight is all about aliveness—coming alive to the intimacy possible between God and each one of us, entering into a life of transforming discipleship with Jesus, experiencing the profound renewal that comes from being alone with God, sharing God's mission of healing with the world, and entering into that sacred mystery of death and resurrection with Christ. Should the Spirit of God breathe this aliveness into your life through your engagement with this book, I will be deeply grateful.

A WORD OF ENCOURAGEMENT

As you read the meditation for each week, I encourage you to engage with the small-group exercises designed to accompany them found at the back of this book. Entering into the abundant life Christ offers demands much more than reading words; it requires participation in actions designed to bring our minds and bodies into interaction with the living God. Without this intentional partnership, Jesus' invitations remain words on paper. But when we open his invitations, explore them, and respond to them, our everyday lives overflow with God's immediacy and power.

Wonderings

RESPONDING TO JESUS' INVITATIONS TEACHES US
HOW TO LIVE MORE FULLY.

Have you ever received an invitation that you lost, discarded,
or to which you failed to respond?
What sense of loss did you experience with the realization
that you missed an invitation?
What does it look like to live life fully alive?

———————————— ≈ ————————————

JESUS INVITES US INTO LIFE AT ITS VERY BEST.

What would life at its very best look like for you?
How does Jesus encourage you to accept his invitation?
Through scripture? friends and family? your community of faith?

Week Two

INVITATION TO TRANSFORMING INTIMACY

Those who love God must love
their brothers and sisters also.

– I JOHN 4:21

Friends, I would like to extend to you an invitation. It is my hope that you will receive this invitation, open it carefully, and explore it in terms of your life at this moment. Simply put, I invite you to fall passionately in love with the God who is passionately in love with us.

Whenever I speak about falling in love with God, I always think of Father Pedro Arrupe. Father Arrupe was elected superior general of the Jesuits in 1965 during the latter part of the Second Vatican Council and at the beginning of a period of massive change in the Catholic church. He would become best known for his strong emphasis on social justice as an essential part of the gospel.

One of my favorite quotes of Father Arrupe has been printed on cards and posters: "Nothing is more practical than finding God, that is, than falling in love in a quite absolute, final way. What you are in love with, what seizes your imagination, will affect everything. It will decide what will get you out of bed in the morning, what you do with your evenings, how you will spend your weekends, what you read, who you know, what breaks your heart, and what amazes you with joy and gratitude. Fall in love, stay in love, and it will decide everything."

However I am also aware that as I share this invitation with you to fall passionately in love with God, you could be muttering under your breath, "Trevor, talking about passion like this is a bit too much." It reminds me of the delightful story of a couple who had been married for fifty years and wanted to rekindle some of the passion of their youths. They were lying in bed together, and the wife said to her husband, "Darling, will you hold me like you used to?" And he did. She then asked, "Will you stroke my hair and my face like you used to?" So he did. She then asked, "Will you nibble my neck like you used to?" He quickly jumped out of bed. "Where are you going?" his wife asked. "I'm just going to the bathroom. I'll get my false teeth and will be back in a moment."

We live in a day and age when it's easy for passion to be drained from of our lives. So many things drain our passion—busyness, strained relationships, heartaches, struggles against injustice, and the overwhelming suffering around us. We easily lose our passion for the lives God has given us. We lose our passion for friendships, relationships, and engagement with others. We lose our passion for our vocations, our ministries, and our daily work. Most tragically of all, we lose our passion for God. Søren Kierkegaard once said, "There will come a day when people will die for lack of passion." Maybe that day has come. It's against this backdrop that I want to extend to you the first invitation—the invitation to transforming intimacy.

A Pharisee, an expert in the Jewish religion, comes to Jesus and asks an important question: "Which commandment in the law is the greatest?" (Matt. 22:36). In effect, he's asking Jesus about the center of Jewish faith. What counts the most? What is the most important aspect of living faithfully for God? Jesus responds, "You shall love the Lord your God with all your heart, and with all your soul, and with all your mind" (22:37). Jesus then does something profoundly radical. He adds a verse from Leviticus: "You shall love your neighbor as yourself" (22:39). Jesus continues, "On these two commandments hang all the law and the prophets" (22:40). Scot McKnight, New Testament scholar, calls this "the Jesus creed." Love God; love neighbor. That's what life is all about.

It is crucial to understand that Jesus is not trying to place a burden on us with these two commandments. When we hear or read them, we tend to think Jesus is trying to lay something heavy on us. We think he's out to spoil our lives—to make our lives harder and a bit more miserable. But that is not the case. Jesus invites us to live into these commandments because he knows what we often forget. He knows that we are created by love, in love, and for love. He knows that we are divinely designed for intimate connection.

Jesus knows that when we live into these commandments, something beautiful begins to happen in our lives. When we embrace these commandments, we begin to find our way back to our true home—the loving heart of God. Most strikingly, by living into Jesus' commands, we become alive again—passionately alive. We become passionately alive to the gift of our own lives, to the sacredness of the person next to us, and to the beauty and brutality of our world. We become alive to Christ, whose presence fills the universe. We become alive to the glory of God that surrounds us and permeates everything there is. Jesus knows this, and that's why he offers to us the invitation to love God and love neighbor.

But sometimes we find it difficult to offer love to God and to our neighbors. I don't know about you, but for almost forty years I have wondered how you can love someone you do not see. As I have lived into this question over the years, there have been some insights that have slowly begun to distill in my heart and mind. I want to share them with you—not as a set formula for how to love God but as an invitation for you to open, explore, and respond to Jesus' invitation to fall passionately in love with the God who is passionately in love with us.

BEING TOUCHED BY GOD'S PASSIONATE LOVE

I am reminded of a true story from Zimbabwe that I love. A number of years ago, the General Secretary of the Bible Society was handing out tracts of the Gospels on the streets of Harare. A young man responded, "I don't want that, and I won't read it." The General Secretary pressed the tract into the young man's hand and said, "Come on. You take it." The young man stated, "I don't want it. And if you give that to me, I'm going to use the paper to make cigarettes." The General Secretary, pressing the tract into the young man's hands, replied, "Take it and do what you want with it."

A year later the General Secretary was preaching in a township just outside of Harare, and who should be there but the young man to whom he had given the tract. "This is a surprise. What are you doing here?" the General Secretary asked. The young man answered him, "You know something? I smoked my way through Matthew. I smoked my way through Mark. I smoked my way through Luke, but when I came to John 3:16, I stopped smoking."

This story reminds us that we fall in love with God when we allow God's passionate desire for us to touch our hearts. At this point, we begin our journey into living the commandments of Jesus. I think this is what the author of First John is also trying to say: "We love because [God] first loved us" (4:19). Or, as that young man from Harare reminds us, we fall in love with God when the life-transforming reality of John 3:16 burns its way into our hearts and minds: "For God so loved the world that he gave his only Son, so that everyone who believes in him may not perish but may have eternal life."

Think a bit about that mind-stretching verse—"For God so loved the world." It vividly reminds us that there is a blazing love at the heart of the universe. This divine energy lies at the core of all things. We see this divine love fully embodied in Jesus Christ. This love calls us by name, pursues us wherever we go, and welcomes us with open arms. It reaches out to each one of us with a crucified love that will never let go.

Has your heart been touched by this love? If it hasn't, I invite you to try a simple practice. Ask the Holy Spirit to make God's love real for you. Pray, "Spirit of God, please make the love of God real for me." I don't know how God's passionate love will come to you, but I know God will take your request seriously.

God's love may come to you in the presence of someone who takes an interest in listening to you. It may come during Holy Communion as you eat the bread and sip the wine. It may come in a beautiful sunset, a moving piece of music, or in the words of scripture. It may come in the depths of your own longings for that which is beyond you and cannot be described in words.

I do not know how God's love will touch you, but this must not stop you from asking for it. Pray, "God, please make your mysterious, intimate, personal love real for me." And when God's love touches your heart, you will begin to fall in love with the One who has loved you from the very beginning.

Staying Faithful in Dark Times

Our love for God grows and deepens when we keep the faith through dark times. When we begin our journey with Christ, we often feel faithful, hopeful, and zealous. Do you remember those days? Jesus feels real and close and near. You feel like you are on honeymoon with God. Then one day God's absence replaces God's presence. This shift is not caused by depression or by despair, and it's not necessarily because you have done anything wrong. It's like something else is going on, as if God is removing a superficial sense of the Divine presence to allow for something deeper to take place in your life.

My spiritual director used to say to me, "Trevor, sometimes God stands at the door of the room of your life and places a hand on the light switch and dims it a bit. Then in the darkness God whispers, 'Will you learn to trust me in the dark? Will you love me even when you don't feel my presence?'" In these moments of darkness, I have found a certain practice very helpful. I have what I call a *love-word* for God that I carry in my heart and repeat when I am in the dark. Often when God feels far away, I say this word to God with all the faith and hope and love in my heart. It has the effect of keeping me consciously connected to God's loving presence even when I do not feel it.

Perhaps a simple analogy from my marriage may help. In the thirty-one years I have been married, there have been some dark moments when all the good feelings seemed to disappear. Like my love-word for God, I have one for my wife, Debbie, too. In those dark moments, I will call her by that name to remind myself of all the deep, good, and beautiful moments we have shared over the years. She knows when I use the word that I'm expressing all my love and longing for her, even though we are experiencing a difficult time together. This simple word keeps us connected through our love for each other even in the darkest of times.

We all need a word like this for God. Can you think of one you might use for the One who passionately loves you? It could be *Abba* or *Beloved* or *My Love* or *Jesus* or something else. In your darkest moments with God, say this word over and over again. Allow it to express your deep desire to remain rooted in the Divine love through the darkness. You may be surprised at how helpful you find this simple practice.

LEARNING TO LOVE OUR NEAREST NEIGHBOR

Our love for God will grow as God's love flows from us to our neighbor: "Those who do not love a brother or sister whom they have seen, cannot love God whom they have not seen" (1 John 4:20).

Notice Jesus does not say we must love everyone. That is God's business. It is impossible for you and me to love everyone in the world. How can we realistically love people we don't know? We are invited to love our *neighbor*, the person or persons nearest to us at the moment. What a relief! We take Jesus' invitation seriously by learning to love those near us. We don't end there, but it is where we begin. We will explore this idea in greater depth in later chapters. For now, let us express our love for God by loving our nearest neighbor. And I assure you, even this will not be easy.

I'll never forget a man in a congregation I once pastored. I will call him Bill. Bill was passionate about God. He would worship with his arms raised, praise God loudly, and pray for ages. He yearned for miracles and revival every Sunday. As his pastor, I often felt inadequate. Miracles and revival every Sunday? That's a lot to ask!

One day I went to visit Bill at his home. He wasn't there, but his wife was. I said to her, "You know, Bill is really passionate about God." She looked at me with fire in her eyes, a look I will never forget. She said, "You can say that. You don't have to live with the man."

Somehow Bill had not made the connection between loving God and loving those closest to him. I do not want to throw stones at Bill. Like Bill, my deepest failings in life have been failings in loving others. I remember the time when I made my ministry work a priority over my wife. Putting work in front of the one you love is a kind of adultery. I will never forget finding a letter as I walked through the door. I have the letter memorized. It read, "Dear Trevor, sometimes it worries me that I won't be worried whether you come home or not. I want to reconnect. Love you, Debbie."

I don't know how things are going for you right now, but I would like to encourage you to try another simple practice. Sometimes in order to open the channels between God and ourselves, we need to confess our failure to love others. Maybe this week tell someone to whom you are very close, "I am sorry for the way I have treated you. I am so sorry. I am sorry for the times I have not listened to you, for the times I have degraded you, for the times I've been sarcastic. I am so sorry, and if there's any way I can make amends, please tell me."

Recently I was at the table in conversation with my children, two young adults in their twenties. In moments such as these when honest and open sharing is involved, your parenting is evaluated. As they talked, I became aware how insensitive I had been to them when they both went through their first relationship breakups. I had been busy going about my own life, and right in front of me, in the lives of my own kids, there were broken hearts. I said to them as we sat together, "Mark, Joni, I'm so sorry."

Maybe you need to confess a particular failure to love someone near you. That confession can lead to greater intimacy. Here is a helpful analogy. Imagine someone sitting at a piano. He or she cannot play music unless the piano lid is lifted. Only then does the person have access to the piano keys. In our relationships, confession opens the piano lid so that God can play music again in our lives. God desires to play music in our lives, but too often our piano lid has been closed by our failures to love others well. Somehow confession has a way of opening the piano so that God can play the notes of joy, laughter, and intimacy in our lives.

RESPONDING

Jesus extends to us the invitation to fall passionately in love with the God who is passionately in love with us. Ask God to touch you with the depth of God's love. If you find yourself in a dark place, choose a love-word for God that expresses your consent for God to do anything God wants in your life. If your dearest relationships have been injured by your own words or actions, make confessions to those persons you have hurt this week.

I believe as we embrace these little practices—of asking God's love to be made real for us, of keeping our love-word for God close to our hearts, and of confessing our failures in loving—we will be surprised by God's passionate love, rich mercy, and deep acceptance. I believe we will find ourselves falling in love again with God.

Wonderings

SØREN KIERKEGAARD ONCE, "THERE WILL COME A DAY WHEN
PEOPLE WILL DIE FOR LACK OF PASSION."

Is today that day for you?
When have you experienced such a lack of passion
that you thought you'd die?

WE WERE DIVINELY DESIGNED FOR INTIMATE CONNECTION.

Do you feel you have forgotten this? How so?
When have you known this statement to be true?

WE BEGIN TO FALL IN LOVE WITH GOD WHEN
OUR LIVES AND HEARTS ARE TOUCHED BY GOD'S
PASSIONATE DESIRE FOR US.

When did you begin falling in love with God?
Have you ever felt God's love touch your heart? In what way?

Week Three

INVITATION TO TRANSFORMING DISCIPLESHIP

As Jesus was walking along, he saw a man called Matthew sitting at the tax booth; and he said to him, "Follow me."

— MATTHEW 9:9

I recently heard the story of an American rancher who believed life's greatest opportunity was to have the biggest and best of everything. He had a bumper sticker on the back of his Hummer that read, "The man with the most toys wins." He made it clear that when he died he wanted to be buried inside his Hummer wearing a tuxedo, while his guests sipped the best champagne. When the man died and it came time to bury him, his coffin was placed inside his Hummer and lowered by crane into the ground. As the coffin was lowered and his guests made a toast with their champagne glasses, one person said to another, "Boy, that's what I call living."

What do you consider life's greatest opportunity? Finding a soul mate? Getting married? Raising kids? Having a good career? Making the world a better place? Exploring and traveling? Having as much fun as possible? My wife, Debbie, would probably say a candlelit dinner with George Clooney.

I do not wish to critique those responses. There are positive aspects to each one. I do, however, want to offer a more radical alternative. Could it be that life's greatest opportunity is the invitation to become a follower of Christ? Or, in the words of Saint Ignatius, the opportunity to come "to know, to love and to serve Jesus Christ." I realize this is an extravagant, bold, and provocative claim. We live in a multifaith, multicultural, multinational world, and I am suggesting a very specific, particular, and unique option. So I want to propose some reasons as to why you might wish to take seriously Christ's invitation to follow him.

Consider the story of Matthew's call in his Gospel account (see Matt. 9:9-13). What reasons undergirded Matthew's wholehearted response to Jesus that day? Dietrich Bonhoeffer tells us that whenever we proclaim a gospel story, Christ has a wonderful way of stepping out of the story and becoming a living Word in the present. I hope Jesus will step out of this Gospel story as we meditate on it and speak into our hearts a life-giving word that evokes a desire to accept, open, and explore the invitation to become a Christ-follower.

Experiencing God's Acceptance

Matthew, a tax collector, accepts the invitation to follow Jesus because he experienced God's unconditional acceptance. We know today that tax collectors were a despised profession, one that excluded them from being part of a respectable community. Matthew would not have been welcomed in the local synagogue. Tax collectors were looked upon as sinners, and Matthew probably considered himself to be utterly unacceptable to God.

Jesus walks into Matthew's world and extends to him some amazing words of invitation: "Follow me" (Matt. 9:9). Imagine how Matthew must have felt in that moment—desired, recognized, and deeply loved. Because he knew Jesus was a prophet, Matthew would have interpreted his invitation as a sign of God's radical and unconditional acceptance.

Henri J. M. Nouwen writes that one of the greatest enemies to the spiritual life is self-rejection. Many of us struggle to know that we are accepted exactly as we are. We have a picture of God deep in our hearts that tells us we are unacceptable unless we jump through certain hoops, meet certain requirements, and fulfill certain demands.

The other day while I was walking through the parking lot of my church, a parishioner approached me and said, "Trevor, I have just been through a divorce. Am I still acceptable to God?" I could hear the anguish in her voice.

How many of us wonder if we are acceptable to God because of who we are, what we've done, or what we've been through? Jesus in his encounter with Matthew disproves the idea that God offers only conditional acceptance. We must hear in the depths of our spirits Christ's whisper, "You are accepted as you are." When we hear these gospel words, we are able—often for the first time in our lives—to accept and even love ourselves. When we hear the words of God's unconditional acceptance, we can embrace the darker and more destructive parts of our lives that we tend to sweep under the rug. It is when we hear these words of acceptance that we can embrace the shadowy sides of our lives and bring them to God because we know we will be accepted as we are. At this point, real change and transformation begins—when we hear Jesus' words of acceptance, we no longer have to pretend. We can take off our religious masks and be who we are. We can sing "Just as I am, without one plea, . . . O lamb of God, I come" and mean it.

PARTICIPATING IN GOD' STORY

Consider some of the dominant story lines of Matthew's life before accepting Jesus' invitation to become one of his followers. Matthew was living the life of a tax collector. The vocation of tax collector involved personal enrichment at the expense of others, exploitation and deception, and getting away with as much as one could. Matthew accepts the invitation to become a Christ-follower because Jesus bids him to participate in God's story.

Jesus walked into Matthew's world and said, "Follow me." His words were an invitation to join with others who were living out God's story. Matthew would have already been familiar with this story. From Abraham forward, God had been working to form a community of people through which God could heal and deliver the world. Jesus issues an invitation to participate in God's healing work. When we live in God's story, people begin to matter, evil is overcome with acts of creative goodness, beauty replaces ugliness, and we begin to connect with those who are in pain.

We all long to be part of a story bigger than our own individual stories. Some of the stories we choose to live are not always helpful or good. Maybe in our attempts to become part of something larger than ourselves we sell our souls to a corporate company or identify uncritically with an ideology or political party. Maybe we immerse ourselves in the lives of TV celebrities. We try to fit our lives into a bigger story in so many ways.

Here is an example. One day, I walked into the coffee shop on my church's campus. Behind the counter was a delightful woman who attends services there. As I ordered my morning cup of coffee, we began talking about our television viewing habits.

"Louise, what did you watch last night?" I asked her. She tried to change the subject.

Intrigued by her resistance, I pressed her. "Come on, Louise, what were you watching last night?"

"I can't tell you, Trevor," she said.

"Come on, what were you watching last night?" I asked.

"I was watching the story of the Playboy mansion," she said.

"That's interesting, can you tell me why?" I asked.

"My life is just so boring. If only I could have one day in the mansion," she replied.

I tell that story because it reveals our deep human need to connect our little story with a bigger story that will hopefully bring greater meaning and purpose to our lives. Tragically, many of the stories we choose to become part of don't do this. They leave us empty, disillusioned, and restless. We need to follow Jesus into God's story—the story for which we were created.

My life was ambushed by Jesus at age sixteen. Almost immediately, I found myself drawn into God's story of liberating and healing the world. Living in this story has transformed my life and given it a profound meaning that I treasure deeply.

LIVING GOD'S WAY

We find much of Jesus' teaching in Matthew's Gospel. In Matthew's account of the Sermon on the Mount, Jesus outlines a breathtaking moral vision for human life that we find nowhere else (see Matt. 5–7). Matthew also records Jesus' parables that contain significant insight into how God moves and works among us. More than any other Gospel writer, Matthew repeats Jesus' teaching about what it means to go on a journey into servanthood.

One blessing of being a pastor is the privilege of getting to know all kinds of people. I have worked in a small, rural town in the South African city of Johannesburg and in the soggy suburbs of large, sprawling residential areas. In each of these settings I learned that deep in the heart of every human being is this question: How do I live well? While these specific words are seldom used, this question is written in the emptiness of our daily lives. It is written on our boredom, our despair, our depression, our experimentation with drugs, our addictions, our compulsions, and all the wreckage of human life that surrounds us. In all these areas we hear the haunting question: How do I live well?

In South Africa, the residents wrestle with this question on a national level. Peter Storey writes, "South Africa is thrashing around in search for its soul." Storey believes that we lack strong values to govern our behavior toward one another. He encourages us to recover an ethical framework for our attitudes toward work, money, sexuality, and power. If the widening economic gap between the *haves* and the *have-nots* is to be bridged, Storey believes we need a large dose of selflessness. "In short," he states, "we need again to learn the difference between right and wrong."

How do I live well? I too ask this question. How do I live freely and joyfully? How do I relate to those close to me? How do I respond to those who disagree with me? How do I love others? How do I contribute to the common good? How do I live with privilege in a country characterized by inequality?

I have discovered that Christ meets us in the midst of these questions and helps us to live into creative responses. It is not so much a matter of asking, "What would Jesus do?" It's about following Jesus, getting to know him, and letting his teaching influence our lives. When we follow Jesus in this way, we are transformed inwardly. We receive new ways of listening and seeing, being attentive and aware, thinking and feeling. Matthew followed Jesus because Jesus showed him God's way to live. This is why I follow him too, and it is why I invite you to consider Jesus' invitation to transforming discipleship. He enables us to live well.

CONNECTING WITH GOD'S POWER

Matthew's Gospel was written after Jesus' death. At that time, no one would have wanted to follow a crucified and dead messiah. But Matthew believed with all his heart that God had raised Jesus from the dead, and Matthew had, in his dealings with Jesus, experienced some of that same resurrecting power. Matthew accepts the invitation to become a Christ-follower because Jesus connected him to God's power.

To become the people we long to be, we need to experience a power from beyond ourselves. Human life is not designed to run on its own resources alone. Recovering alcoholics and addicts will say this is one of the biggest lessons they learn through their own rehabilitation. They need a power beyond themselves in order to embrace the journey to freedom. Speaking from my own heart, I long to be a better person, someone who is more loving, more caring, more honest and true, and more responsive to those in need. I long to be delivered from my own deceptions, deceit, and duplicity.

Each week Debbie and I have supper with a group of seven young couples with whom we reflect on life and discipleship within the challenging reality of South Africa. Our meals together are a journey in spiritual formation through conversation. I am the one charged with bringing home dinner. One night as I waited to pick up some pizzas from a fast-food restaurant, a homeless man approached me. I began talking to him. I asked him about his life— where he was from and where he lived. He asked me questions too, and I shared some parts of my life story with him. As I was about to go, he asked, "Do you have some money for me?" I told him I only had a credit card. The truth, however, was that I had cash in my back pocket.

There I was, a follower of Jesus for over forty years, and I could not speak the truth to a homeless man. Why could I not just say, "I'm sorry. I don't give money to everyone"? Why could I not be honest? I arrived at the group meeting with our food, and as I walked into the room I told them what had happened at the restaurant and asked for their prayers. We began talking about our deception in our dealings with those who are economically disadvantaged. Why do we lie? Why do we not tell the truth about our wealth and what we have? Why are we so dishonest?

Let me be blunt: We need a power from beyond ourselves to help us let go of our addictions to deception and duplicity. The good news is that the more we engage with Jesus, the more we will find ourselves gradually empowered by God's resurrection power. Like Matthew, we will get up.

Maybe a day will come when if asked by someone who is homeless for money, I will tell the truth because I trust in God's power. When I look back over my life, I can see little moments of deliverance and freedom. This is why I follow Jesus. I may still be a mess now, but I cannot imagine the mess I would be without the resurrecting power of Christ in my life.

Life's greatest opportunity is Jesus' invitation to transforming discipleship. Jesus invites us to participate in God's story. He shows us how to live God's way. He connects us with God's power. But most of all, when we become Christ-followers, we experience God's unconditional acceptance.

One of the greatest influences on my life is the philosopher Dallas Willard. Dallas was on faculty in the philosophy department at the University of Southern California. Those of you who have spent time in a philosophy department know this is where the cynics often convene. One day a young Ph.D. student came to Dallas and said, "Dallas, you are a smart man. Why do you follow Jesus?" Philosophers answer questions with questions, so Dallas asked the student, "Tell me young man, who else do you have in mind?"

Wonderings

JESUS WALKED INTO MATTHEW'S WORLD
AND SAID, "FOLLOW ME."

When have you heard that invitation?
When have you felt desired, recognized, wanted, and loved?

———— ≈ ————

REAL CHANGE AND TRANSFORMATION BEGIN WHEN WE HEAR
JESUS' WORDS OF ACCEPTANCE.

When did your transformation begin? Or has it yet to begin?
What would it take for you to hear Jesus' words of acceptance?
What masks would you like to take off today?

———— ≈ ————

ONE OF OUR DEEPEST NEEDS IS TO BECOME THE PEOPLE
WE LONG TO BE.

Who do you long to be?

Week Four

INVITATION
TO
TRANSFORMING
SOLITUDE

And the Spirit immediately drove [Jesus] out

into the wilderness.

— MARK 1:12

Ayoung man who wanted to incorporate solitude and silence into his life joined the strictest Trappist monastery he could find. That particular monastery allowed its monks to speak one sentence every ten years. After the young man had been there ten years, the abbot called him into his study and asked, "What would you like to say?" The young man replied, "Could I have bran flakes in the morning rather than whole wheat cereal?" The abbot said, "I will see to that." The young man went back into silence. Ten more years passed. The abbot asked, "What would you like to say?" "Do you mind if I have a softer mattress?" the man asked. "Fine," the abbot replied. The man returned to silence once again. When thirty years had passed the abbot asked, "What would you like to say?" He said to the abbot, "I've had enough of this. I'm leaving." The abbot replied, "I'm not surprised; you're always complaining!"

I vividly remember the moment I first experienced transforming solitude. I was twenty-nine years old. A number of events converged in my life that year. I got married, an immensely transitional moment for me. I was working in downtown Johannesburg in a mission church. It was a very dark and difficult time in South Africa's history, and I had to discern what faithfulness to Christ meant. That same year, together with forty-one other people, I had my first experience of a South African jail for taking part in an illegal march protesting the detention of a man without trial. For a young, white, privileged South African, it was a shock to my system.

I will never forget the Sunday at church following our release from jail. I learned we had lost about one-third of our members in a single week. It was a turbulent time for me. I was trying to cope with my marriage, my ministry, my stint in jail, and the people leaving the church. Life was chaotic both internally and externally. I knew I needed help that only God could give. I found my way to a Dominican retreat center in Johannesburg and knocked on the door. A nun dressed in blue jeans answered, welcomed me, and led me to the little room that would be my home for the next three days. The room contained a bed, a crucifix, and a chair. As she left me she said, "Trevor, if you need anything, just give me a shout, and I will show you how to live without it."

Later the nun gave me a passage of scripture—John 7:37-39. It became my friend over the next three days. There were times when I became fidgety and wanted to go home. But I learned something during those days that I have not forgotten: If we want to advance in God's purposes for our lives, we must first retreat.

With this in mind, I invite you into transforming solitude. This invitation is intrinsically rooted in the life of Jesus. I encourage you to read one of the Gospels all the way through in a single sitting. When you do, you will begin to notice certain things about Jesus' life. For example, in Mark's Gospel, you will notice straightaway that

Mark portrays Jesus as a man of action. As you follow Jesus through the village of Galilee, he's always on the go, proclaiming the reign of God; teaching the parables; healing people in body, mind, and spirit; releasing people from the power of evil; feeding the hungry; forming a small mission team; building friendships; and confronting religious authorities. The list of Jesus' activities goes on and on and on.

You will also notice that many moments of solitude and silence undergird Jesus' active life. His whole life is punctuated by these empty spaces. In Mark 1:12, Jesus goes into the wilderness. Later, that same chapter gives a detailed description of a day in Jesus' life. After a full day's ministry, Jesus rises early the next morning to go to a solitary place and pray (see Mark 1:35-39). In Mark 6, Jesus calls a few friends together to go to a quiet place and rest. In Mark 9, Jesus takes three of his closest friends to a mountain where they experience the overwhelming presence of God.

The invitation from Mark's Gospel is clear: If we are going to be followers of Christ, if we are going to walk in his way and be formed by him, then we need to receive, open, and explore Jesus' invitation to transforming solitude. We must learn what it means to retreat in order to advance. I would like to share some of the transforming gifts that come in moments of solitude and silence. I speak on the basis of experience—both my own and others'—and also from what I have learned from scripture.

REST

The first transforming gift is the gift of rest, refreshment, and renewal. Recall the story of Elijah in 1 Kings 18–19. Elijah defeats the prophets of Baal, calls down fire from heaven, and prays successfully for rain in the middle of a drought. Despite his success, Elijah collapses in despair because of Jezebel's threat to destroy him.

Elijah takes refuge under a broom tree where he falls asleep only to be awakened by an angel who brings him food and drink. Elijah eats and drinks and goes back to sleep. When he wakes once more, he finds food and drink by his side again. Only after rest and renewal is Elijah prepared for an encounter with God.

Elijah travels forty days to Mount Horeb to meet God. On the mountain, God comes to him and asks Elijah, "What are you doing here?" Notice what Elijah does next—he pours out to God his sense of shattering failure, his puzzlement and pain, his despair and desperation (see 1 Kings 19:14). After he does this, he is recommissioned by God to participate in God's work in the world.

Elijah's story reminds me of the New Testament account of Jesus and Peter in John 21. The two stories are quite similar when you think about the sense of failure Peter must have felt, the long conversation between Jesus and himself, the food, Jesus' question to Peter, "Do you love me?", and Peter's recommissioning at the end of the story (see vv. 4-19).

Elijah's story is full of practical, pastoral, and psychological wisdom. We also need a restful place under a broom tree. We need a place of retreat where we can sleep, eat, and be refreshed physically. We need a place where we can pour out our puzzlement, pain, and sense of failure to God—all the feelings we can't pour out when we're meeting deadlines at work, picking up kids from school, and sitting in traffic. Like Elijah, we need a place where we can hear God speak words that humble us and trim our egos, until ultimately, like Elijah and Peter, we too can be recommissioned into ministry.

Do you have such a place? My first broom tree was in Johannes-burg with a Catholic order called "The Little Sisters of Jesus." The Sisters owned a house in a predominantly Muslim community. In the rear of the house was a room where I would go once a month to sleep and eat and pour my heart out to God. I still remember going to this little room at three o'clock in the morning after my first child was born. The room was my broom tree where angels could minister to me like they did to Elijah. Do you have a place under the broom tree where you can receive the transforming gift of rest, refreshment, and renewal?

NOT BEING ALONE

The second transforming gift we discover in solitude is the knowl-edge that we are not alone. Serving as a pastor is a tremendous priv-ilege. I have learned much more from human encounters than from any pastoral textbook. What I've learned from being with people is that nearly every human being lives with a deep loneliness.

Loneliness manifests itself in different ways. There is the lone-liness of losing someone you love, of going through a divorce, of a friendship breaking up, or of being a young mother. There is the loneliness of leadership when you lead an organization and hold a position of responsibility. There is the loneliness of carrying the secrets of shameful and destructive actions you may have taken.

We all carry a loneliness of some kind, and we experience this loneliness whether we are young or old, male or female, rich or poor. Loneliness may be the deepest kind of suffering in our world. Henri J. M. Nouwen experienced a profound loneliness during his life and explored that pain through his books. He discovered that when our loneliness is embraced in God's presence, it can be healed and transformed into a life-giving solitude. Still, this is not an easy journey.

A minister once went to see Carl Jung, the famous psychiatrist. He was burned-out, broken, and weary. Jung said to him, "Every night for a week, when your day is over, I want you to go into your study and be alone." On Monday night, the minister closed the door of his study and listened to music. On Tuesday, he wrote some letters. On Wednesday, he caught up on work, and so the week unfolded. He returned to the famous psychiatrist looking terrible. Jung asked, "How was it?"

"It was horrible," the man answered.

Jung asked, "What did you do?" When the minister explained how he had spent the week, Jung said, "I didn't ask you to do that. I asked you to be on your own."

"I can't stand my own company!" the minister exclaimed.

Jung replied, "You are forcing the company you can't stand on everyone else, eighteen hours a day."

When we enter into solitude, we must do so with a simple trust that the one who calls us into the solitude will meet us there. God will not leave us alone. In the silence, you will hear the Divine voice say, "You are my beloved. You are mine." This has happened for many of Christ's followers, and it can happen for you and me when we open our lives to the invitation of transforming solitude.

I was once at a large denominational church conference in the United States where I had little interaction with the actual conference itself. I stayed in a hotel, was transported to the conference at ten o' clock in the morning where I spoke, and then immediately returned to my hotel room. I lived this way for three days, and it was a very lonely experience. By the third night, I was feeling down. I struggled to turn the loneliness into solitude. While showering that evening, I said to God, "Lord, do you know I am here? I sense you don't know I am in this place! Please let me know you know I am here." I came out of the shower and saw the little red light blinking on my cell phone. It was three o'clock in the morning in South Africa, and I immediately became anxious.

When I opened the text message, I saw it was from Debbie. It read, "Trevor, I can't sleep and I just want you to know that I wish you were here so I could hug you." It was a God moment for me. You might be thinking what a cool coincidence this was, but no! I asked my daughter who is an actuary specializing in statistics what the statistical probability of getting a text message like the one from Debbie at three o'clock in the morning would be. About 0.00001! I believe that God said to me that evening through Debbie, "Trevor, I know you're there." In my loneliness I discovered the transforming gift of not being alone.

DISCOVERING GOD'S COMPASSIONATE HEART

The third gift is discovering God's compassionate heart. "Be still, and know that I am God!" (Ps. 46:10). There are three parts to this short sentence—stillness, knowledge, and God. All three go together.

There are at least two kinds of knowledge. First, there is knowledge *about* something. When I speak with my fellow ministry colleagues in South Africa, we often talk about the wonderful accessibility in the United States to resources of knowledge about God, prayer, spiritual formation, ministry, and mission. What an incredible gift!

The second kind of knowledge comes from personal interaction. For example, you know a little bit about my wife, Debbie, from what I have told you already. You know she is married to a guy named Trevor. You know she would love to have a candlelight dinner with George Clooney. I can also tell you that she is a biology teacher who has given her life to education. You know these facts about her. You do not, however, personally know her love, anger, grace, compassion, and capacity to forgive. These things I know because they come from my intimate interaction with her. Similarly, in the silence there is a personal knowledge of God that comes to us from our direct and intimate interaction with God. In intimate silence with God, we come to know God's compassionate heart for the world, not just about it.

If you came to South Africa and worshipped in one of our township churches, you would notice that often no organ accompanies the choir. There is only a conductor. If you watch carefully before worship begins, the conductor strikes a tuning fork against a table. The choir is quiet, still, and aware. They are listening for the note on the tuning fork.

God has struck the earth with a tuning fork named Jesus. The sound we hear is the sound of God's compassion for the world. We hear it in the solitude, the silence, and the stillness. In the silence, we receive a new awareness of the world. When we turn our eyes upon Jesus and look into his face as the hymn invites us, all the things of the world do not grow strangely dim; they become clearer. The beauty and the brutality of the world become clearer in the light of the glory and grace of Jesus. In the solitude and silence we are fueled by a deeper compassion—God's compassion—for others.

In South Africa, 1976 was a big year. On June 16, townships became frenzied as students took to the streets in protest against the educational system. Two months before, Desmond Tutu had been on silent retreat. In the silence, he began to sense in a new way the urgency of the oppressive educational system in South Africa. From a place of retreat Tutu wrote a letter to the prime minister asking him—begging him—to act in a different way. The letter warned the prime minister that the streets were going to erupt in protest. Tutu's letter was ignored.

We come to see the world more clearly in silence and solitude. Tutu's prophetic glimpse came to him in solitude. It is in solitude that I can see my marriage more clearly. In solitude I can better see how I am living, how I have hurt people, and how I need to make amends. Perhaps you have experienced these insights in silence and solitude as well.

I invite you to open yourself to receive the transforming gifts of solitude—rest, refreshment, and renewal—that you may be recommissioned to participate in God's mission. I invite you into the discovery that you are not on your own. I invite you to enter into a personal knowledge of God's compassionate heart through intimate interaction with God in the silence. I invite you to begin stepping into this experience. Start with short moments of solitude. Don't try and fill the moments, just leave them empty. Maybe you take an hour to sit and do nothing but be with God.

Henri J. M. Nouwen writes, "Solitude is the furnace of transformation." Ask Christ to be with you as you take your first step into solitude. Open yourself to receive Christ's invitation to transforming solitude and let him show you the way.

Wonderings

ACCEPTING THE INVITATION TO TRANSFORMING SOLITUDE
IS RETREATING IN ORDER TO ADVANCE.

When have you felt the need to retreat in order to advance?
How have you experienced silence and solitude in your life?

———————— ≈ ————————

THE FIRST GIFTS OF SOLITUDE ARE REST, REFRESHMENT,
AND RENEWAL.

Have you ever received those gifts in solitude?
Where might you find a sacred space or place of retreat?

———————— ≈ ————————

IN SOLITUDE, WE DISCOVER THAT WE ARE NOT ALONE.

What is your greatest loneliness?
How might you find companionship in solitude?

Week Five

Invitation
to
Transforming
Mission

"Lord, teach us to pray...."

– LUKE 11:1

Once in a small Texas town, some social entrepreneurs came together to build a bar. They decided to build it directly across from the local church. Instead of seeing this as a wonderful opportunity to engage in transforming mission right outside their door, the leaders of the church became angry and began to pray passionately that God would intervene. One night, as the bar was under construction, there was a terrible storm. The building was struck by lightning and destroyed. The church leaders were delighted with the turn of events, and the owners of the bar were angry. They decided to sue the church because they knew the congregation had been praying for God to prevent the bar's construction. In court, the church leaders denied they had anything to do with the storm. The judge presiding over the case said, "I have never come across anything like this in my life. Here we have some bar owners who believe in the power of prayer and a whole church that doesn't!"

This story makes me wonder if we really believe what we are praying when we pray the Lord's Prayer—or any prayer for that matter. Would you agree that to believe something is to act as if it were true? To believe the Lord's Prayer and to pray it means we embody it;

indeed, we become the Lord's Prayer. Shane Claiborne says it best when he writes, "Prayer is not so much convincing God to do what we want God to do, as it is convincing ourselves to do what God wants us to do." God wants us to live the Lord's Prayer just as Jesus lived it. This is what it means to be part of God's mission in our world today.

So here is the invitation I wish for us to consider: Will you and I sign up to become participants in God's world-transforming mission? We do not have a mission separate from God's mission. God is looking for people who will bear God's healing and loving presence into the world. Are you willing to receive this invitation, open it, and explore it in terms of your own life right now? I believe the best way to participate in God's mission in the world is to learn how to live the Lord's Prayer. This is what Jesus did, and we are called to do it as well. What does this invitation mean for you and me?

DEEPENING INTIMACY WITH GOD

Before living out the Lord's Prayer, we must first deepen our intimacy with God. Transforming mission arises out of profound intimacy with a God who is both good and loving. Jesus taught the disciples to pray saying, "Father." How do you picture God? The image we have of God powerfully shapes our experience of God. Many of us have a default picture in our minds of a God who is against us. When things go wrong we tend to see God as punishing us or trying to teach us a lesson. This picture of God makes intimacy impossible.

I'm reminded of a story about a child who wouldn't eat his prunes. The child's mother said, "You better eat your prunes, or God will punish you." The child was adamant that he was not going to eat his prunes, so his mother sent him to his room. While in his room there came a massive thunderstorm outside. The boy walked to his window and said, "Such a fuss over five prunes!"

Some of us picture in our minds a God who makes a fuss over five prunes. It is hard to have an intimate relationship with a God who only seeks to punish us. For this reason, the primary task of those who teach and preach is to present a God who is loving, gracious, and merciful.

But there is another reason why our picture of God is so important. Inevitably, we will become like the God we worship. If we worship a God who includes certain people and excludes others, we too will include certain people and exclude others. If we have a picture of God who is on the side of South Africa and against all other nations or on the side of America and against all other nations, it will influence the way we respond to the people of other nations. If our God is violent and aggressive, we too will be violent and aggressive.

In the Gospels, Jesus introduces us to Abba, a good and loving God who makes the sun shine upon the good and evil alike, a God who allows the rain to fall on the righteous and the unrighteous. Jesus' whole life and mission was rooted in a profound intimacy with his heavenly parent. Albert Nolan, a South African theologian, underscores Jesus' relationship with God when he writes, "It is impossible to understand why and how Jesus did the things he did without [his] intimacy with Abba." It follows that if we are going to become participants in God's transforming mission, we too will need to find our way into an intimate relationship with Jesus' Abba.

SHARING LIFE TOGETHER

We participate in God's transforming mission when we share life together as a beloved community. Notice the pronouns in the Lord's Prayer—*us* and *our*. Gospel life is life together. Even in solitude and silence, we are part of this *us* and *our*. We cannot say, "Jesus, I love you, and I want you, but I don't like your family, especially Mr. So-and-So who should go join the church down the road." When Christ enters our lives, he comes to us with his arms around his brothers and sisters—all his brothers and sisters. This is the image I would love for us to have in sharing life together in Jesus.

Sharing life together in Jesus means we are part of a diverse family. I was particularly struck by this reality a few years ago when I took a month-long break from preaching, and Debbie and I decided to visit a few other churches. We worshipped first with the Anglicans. The service was beautifully ordered—the smells, bells, and robes. When the priest put the chalice to my lips, I could taste Christ's presence. The following week we worshipped with the Pentecostals. We stood singing for forty-five minutes, and Christ was present there too. After that we went to the Quaker church, and do you know what Quakers do? Nothing. They simply sit in silence for an hour. But I could feel Christ's presence in the gathered silence. The fourth week Debbie told me to go on my own, so I went to the Methodist church. Do you know what it's like there? It is a little like a Dagwood sandwich—hymn, prayer, hymn, prayer, hymn, prayer, hymn, sermon, hymn. And Jesus was there too!

When we share life together, we must share it honestly. Transforming mission happens when we share life together in the midst of our differences. Too often church is the last place in town where you can be really honest. I sense a deep resistance toward the church among younger generations, and this could be one reason why. They like who Jesus was but want nothing to do with church. Are we in touch with this resistance towards church? Do we listen to the stories of those who find church a hypocritical and dishonest place? What keeps our churches from being places where we can share our lives honestly and deeply and know that we will be accepted as we are?

Many recovery groups meet at the church where I pastor. Sometimes I stop by the Alcoholics Anonymous gathering to listen and observe. It can be really messy in there. Someone might stand and say, "This week has been terrible. I slipped back into my old habits." Someone else might stand and say, "It's been a horrible week. I have been ugly to my kids and hard to live with."

A Bible study group meets in the fellowship hall next door to the AA room. People sit in a circle and are polite. Sometimes I wonder where Jesus hangs out in this church. Is he in the AA room or the fellowship hall? I have a hunch that Jesus hangs out mostly in the AA room because that is where the messes and muddles of life are being shared with honesty. It is where transforming mission is taking place in community. I invite you to allow God to use you to form beloved community where you are—a place where people can take off their masks, be open about their struggles, and learn to live in the light with one another.

ENGAGING THE SUFFERING AROUND US

On a personal level, transforming mission engages the suffering around us. When Jesus calls God *Abba*, it does not signify some cozy relationship he has with the Creator of the universe. This is vocational language. Jesus is aligning himself with the love, transformation, healing, and redemption of the world his Abba is actively involved in right now. When Jesus hears the words, "This is my Son, the Beloved" (Matt. 17:5), it means there is work to be done. And if this is what it meant for Jesus, then it must also mean the same for us.

When we pray the Lord's Prayer, we must ask ourselves if we are actively living out each petition. When we say, "Your kingdom come. Your will be done, on earth as it is in heaven" (Matt. 6:10), we are saying to God, "Sign us up; recruit us; enlist us in bringing heaven to earth." In 2011, a man named Harold Camping made a prediction about the end of the world. Camping got it wrong in a number of ways. The date he had predicted came and passed without the world ending. We should not be surprised. God is not in the business of snatching us away to heaven. God is in the business of bringing heaven to earth in the here and now. God wants all of us to take part in bringing heaven to earth in whatever way we can, no matter what stage of life we are in. Let me explain what I mean.

Not long ago I read *Tales of Wonder*, the autobiography of Huston Smith, a well-known professor of religion and philosophy. He became famous in the United States in 1995 when he appeared with Bill Moyers on a PBS program about comparative religions. He is ninety-four years old, and due to his ill health, he lives in an assisted living facility. Near the end of the book, he writes, "People go to nursing homes, I have heard it said, to die. I came to this assisted living residence, it seems, to cheer people up. Every morning I mentally take a census of every other resident here. And as each person appears in my imagination, I ask myself and God how I can improve his or her day." This is transforming mission. No matter how old we become, we are never too old to embody the words "Your kingdom come. Your will be done, on earth as it is in heaven."

When we pray, "Give us this day our daily bread" (Matt. 6:11), we are saying to God, "Sign us up; recruit us; enlist us in God's bread-for-the-world movement." A pastor friend in Durban, South Africa, noticed that some homeless people had started coming to worship at his church on Sunday evenings. They sat in the back row, unwashed, poorly clothed, and often smelling of alcohol. My friend went to the church leaders to express his interest in reaching out to them. The church decided to buy six round tables to place in the hall on Sundays before the evening service. Now, members of the congregation and the homeless individuals sit together enjoying food, conversation, and fellowship. Gradually people are learning names, sharing stories, and even becoming friends. This is what it means to embody the Lord's Prayer. This is what participating in God's transforming mission is all about.

When we pray, "Forgive us our debts, as we also have forgiven our debtors" (Matt. 6:12), we are saying to God, "Sign us up; recruit us; enlist us in your work of reconciliation in the world." Desmond Tutu says there is no future for the human race without forgiveness. There is no future for America or for South Africa or for any other part of the world without forgiveness. Let us work to break cycles of hurt and hatred with actions of forgiving love as we become part of God's movement of reconciliation.

My wife, Debbie, teaches in a government school in South Africa. She has given her life to this educational work. In one of her classes she said to her students, "I would love to hear your dreams." One fifteen-year-old girl raised her hand and said, "My dream is that all the teachers in this school will be killed." Debbie came home that night traumatized by the experience. We talked about it as a family and reflected on how she might respond in a way that would reflect transforming mission.

The next day Debbie made it her job to learn the girl's name. Her name was Lerato. Each morning Debbie greeted her by name. After three months, they had a conversation at break time. Debbie asked her, "Can you tell me something about your life?" Lerato shared with her the trauma of growing up in desperate poverty in South Africa. Lerato's story was a moment of shared human understanding. Before writing this chapter, I asked Debbie how Lerato is doing. She said Lerato has become one of the most participative learners in the classroom. Transforming mission happens in the classroom, at work, at home, in the assisted living center—it happens right where we are.

Transforming mission engages the suffering of those around us. Transforming mission is about making God's love real in the world. Transformation emerges from a profound intimacy with the good and loving God. Transforming mission happens when we share life with each other in honesty and depth—our pain, our brokenness, our struggles, our temptations, our joys, our laughter, and our food. Do we truly believe the Lord's Prayer? To believe something is to act as if it were so. If we do believe, then for God's sake let us become it.

Wonderings

TO BELIEVE IN SOMETHING IS TO ACT AS IF IT WERE TRUE.

Do you believe the Lord's Prayer?

How do you live out the Lord's Prayer in your daily life?

———————— ≈ ————————

TO ACCEPT JESUS' INVITATION, WE NEED TO SEEK
AN INTIMATE RELATIONSHIP WITH GOD—JESUS' ABBA.

What does God look like for you—a loving parent? an angry Creator?
something in between?

———————— ≈ ————————

TRANSFORMING MISSION OCCURS WHEN WE SHARE LIFE
TOGETHER IN THE MIDST OF OUR DIFFERENCES.

When have you experienced God outside your community of faith?
Where are you called to make God's love real in the world?

Week Six

Invitation to Transforming Mystery

[Some Greeks] came to Philip . . . and said to him,

"Sir, we wish to see Jesus."

– JOHN 12:21

In John 12, some Greeks approach Philip to make a simple request: they want to see Jesus. They had heard about Jesus but now wanted to see him. The distinction is important. They wanted to go from a secondhand-knowing to a firsthand-knowing of Jesus—from knowing about Jesus to knowing Jesus personally. This is usually a lifelong journey. We know a lot about Jesus through listening to sermons, attending Sunday school classes, and reading scripture, but coming to know him through a personal, interactive relationship is very different.

Philip goes to Andrew, and Andrew and Philip go to Jesus with the request. You might expect Jesus to say, "Great! Bring them here. Let them see me for themselves." But he doesn't. Instead Jesus responds in an intriguing way. He offers an image of a seed being planted in the ground and dying. He speaks about losing your life in order to find it. He addresses the issue of sacrificial servanthood. Talk about an indirect response!

In the different threads of Jesus' answer, we discover the invitation to live into the transforming mystery of the gospel. When we do not live into this mystery, we miss out on experiencing God, Christ, and the Holy Spirit. Let us hold the invitation of this mystery before us in our hearts and minds. As we do so, maybe the Spirit will grant the desires of our hearts to participate in this mystery and experience the transformation it can bring about in our lives.

DYING AND RISING

When Jesus spoke about a seed that is planted in the ground and then dies, he was referring primarily to his own death. He would pour out his life for others on the cross. At first, his death would look like a tragedy, but in the end it would be a triumph. It would look like defeat but would really be a victory. Jesus' death would ultimately be the triumph of the resurrection power of God's self-giving love over the forces of sin, evil, and death. This is why Christians say, "Christ has died, Christ is risen, Christ will come again." We often call this proclaiming "the mystery of faith."

This mystery is unique to Jesus. We cannot do what he did. But Jesus invites us to share in a different part of the mystery. Like a seed that is planted in the ground and dies, we are invited to die in order to live. This is the gospel secret expressed by Jesus. If we want to become alive to ourselves, to others, to the world, to God, to Jesus, and to the Spirit, we must let go. We must lay down our lives for God and for others in order to be raised to life.

Let me be clear. When Jesus spoke like this, he was not trying to lay heavy burdens on our lives. He was describing reality. Richard

Rohr says that God always comes to us disguised as reality. Jesus was describing the reality of how life works. It's like a math teacher who stands in the classroom and says to his students, "Unless you learn arithmetic, you cannot do algebra." The teacher is not being nasty or unfair to the students. The teacher is describing reality. We can embrace it or fight it. When we embrace it, we are transformed.

AN EVERYDAY MYSTERY

We have opportunities to embrace Jesus' transforming mystery in our everyday lives. Henri J. M. Nouwen once said that human life is a series of losses. We experience loss constantly. We are born, and we lose the security of the womb. We go to school, and we lose the familiarity of home. We go to work, and we lose the carefree days of youth. We get married and have children, and we lose the freedom of being single. We die, and we lose it all! These are just some of the losses we will experience during our lives. Each one presents us with a choice. We can either clench our fists to hold on to the old, or we can open our hands and let go. Letting go opens us to the unimagined newness that God wants to bring to our lives.

Many of us may experience other kinds of loss—the loss of innocence through abuse, the loss of intimacy through betrayal, the loss of marriage through divorce, the loss of health through sickness, the loss of work through retrenchment, the loss of confidence through failure, and the list goes on and on. Perhaps you are experiencing one of these losses right now.

All of these painful experiences represent a kind of death. Either we hold on to the old, clench our fists, and say, "I'm not going to let go," or we open our hands, embrace the mystery of the moment, and trust that God is a God of resurrection presence and unimagined newness. God is always present, always seeking to bring about the new from the old. We must keep before us the mystery of faith— Christ has died, Christ is risen, Christ will come again.

I remember when my children left home. My daughter was the first to go. I can still remember the day. She was eighteen years old. It was her last day of school, and she was going to spend three months in London. I took her to Oliver Tambo Airport, and as she walked through that exit door, my heart cracked. There was my little girl who had once crawled into my lap, listened to bedtime stories, and danced in my arms. Now she was leaving to explore the city of London by herself. It was a moment of dying for me and learning to be open to the new and unknown.

In order to ritualize this new opportunity, I wrote a prayer and sent it to my daughter. I gave the same prayer to my son two years later when he left home to work overseas for a year. This is what I wrote: "I believe that you were created to live freely, and I place your life now into the hands of your loving Creator. I let go of my clinging hold on your life, and I'm willing for you now to make your own choices. I respect the image of God in you. I want to learn to love you with open hands. I love you, and I bless you. I have confidence in you, and I always will."

Are you living with clenched fists or open hands? Remember what Jesus told us: Hold on to your life and lose it, lose your life and find it. It is this transforming mystery of the gospel into which you and I are invited.

CHOOSING THE MYSTERY

We can choose to live in the transforming mystery of the gospel and allow it to become a daily spiritual practice. Each day we can choose to give our lives away in sacrificial servanthood. Look again at John 12:20-26. Notice how Jesus joins several different themes into one mystery. He talks about a seed being planted, about losing your life in order to find it, and about servanthood. All three themes are part of the transforming mystery of the gospel—the dying and the rising, losing and finding our lives, and serving others.

Perhaps you remember President John F. Kennedy's famous speech in which he proclaimed, "Ask not what your country can do for you—ask what you can do for your country." Historians tell us that these words, spoken with passion and conviction, released an amazing current of sacrificial servanthood that spread around the globe. John F. Kennedy's words described reality at its deepest—we discover life in its fullest when we lay it down for others.

We often resist this transforming mystery and wonder why our marriages, communities, nations, and lives do not work. Let us not hold on to our lives but give them away sacrificially and with joyful abandon. When we step into the transforming mystery of the gospel, the miracle of small resurrections takes place in and around us.

I remember finishing a talk at a retreat center in the United States and noticing that the light of my cell phone was blinking. I had received a message from my family in South Africa. My wife had just taken our dog Pebbles, who had been in our family seventeen years, to be put down at the vet. At that moment, one of the retreatants came up and offered to take me to the airport because she wanted to speak with me about some turmoil in her own life.

The last thing I wanted to do in my grief about Pebbles was listen to someone else's sadness. I knew I had a choice. I prayed to God, *Lord, I need your help. I want to be here now for this person who is driving, but I am finding it very difficult.* As I prayed, I turned to the driver and said, "It would be a privilege to be a witness to what you want to share." She shared something with me that had happened over thirty years ago but had haunted her ever since. Outside the airport I asked if we could pray. I laid my hands on her shoulders and prayed that God would bring about unimagined newness in the midst of her pain.

We will have moments in our lives like this where we have to choose if we will live for ourselves or for others. Knowing that we are beloved by God, we are free to give ourselves away in sacrificial servanthood. E. Stanley Jones, an American missionary to India, once said, "There are two groups of people in this world. There is a very big group of people in this world who are miserable. They live for themselves. There's another group who have given their lives away to others. Their lives are filled with a wild, wild joy."

We are invited to participate in the transforming mystery of the gospel. It invites us to choose between two kinds of death. On the one hand, there is the death that comes from holding and clenching our fists instead of loving and giving and sharing. It's a death that leads to death. On the other hand, there is the death of laying down our lives, giving them away, opening our clenched fists, and surrendering the old. It can be difficult and painful, but it leads to unimagined newness. Which death are you going to choose for your life? My prayer for you is that it will be the death that leads you deeper into the transforming mystery of Jesus Christ.

Wonderings

WE MUST MAKE THE TRANSITION FROM KNOWING
ABOUT JESUS TO KNOWING JESUS PERSONALLY.

Do you know Jesus secondhand from hearing about him,
or do you know him personally?
How have you stepped into the mystery of God?

———————— ≈ ————————

WE CAN EITHER LIVE WITH CLENCHED FISTS
OR WITH OPEN HANDS.

How are you living?
What do you need to let go of in order to embrace new life?

LEADER'S GUIDE

For the next six weeks, you will be facilitating a discussion on *Invitations of Jesus*. Discussion at each weekly gathering will draw from weekly readings and personal engagement of the *Wonderings*.

The weekly readings and responses require thirty to forty minutes a week, and they lead up to and become the starting point for a weekly small-group discussion. This leader's guide includes a plan for an introductory gathering and five weekly gatherings of fifty minutes to an hour and fifteen minutes, depending on whether the group chooses to practice *lectio divina*.

Each gathering will follow a simple and consistent pattern: Opening, Reading the Word, Reflecting on the Invitation, Responding to the Invitation, and Closing.

GATHERING

These six group gatherings are designed for about fifty minutes each. If the group chooses to practice *lectio divina*, the gathering could last an hour and fifteen minutes. The pattern of reading, reflecting, and responding remains the same each week so that participants will, after the first week, know what to expect. The emphasis of each gathering will be conversation together rather than detailed preparation. Sitting in a circle might prove to be most conducive to conversation and discussion.

PREPARING FOR THE GATHERINGS

Leader preparation for each session is minimal; with a Bible, candle, and matches, you can host a meaningful gathering for discussion and prayer. If you wish, you may rotate leadership each week among group participants. If you choose to share the leadership responsibilities, give group participants ample notice about which gathering they will facilitate.

Each week at the beginning of the gathering, light the candle at the center of the group to remind everyone of God's invitation to be present and of God's presence in the group.

LECTIO DIVINA

Lectio divina is a slow, meditative reading and reflection on a passage of scripture. Rather than processing the text intellectually, you're invited to let the words and images connect your heart to God's heart.

Using the weekly selection of scripture, you'll read the text three times, listening for a different aspect each time.

The facilitator will read the scripture the first time. Ask participants to listen for a word or phrase that leaps out at them: "What word or phrase calls to you or sticks in your memory? As you hear the word, gently take it into your heart and silently recite or ponder the word during the silence."

The facilitator or other participant reads the scripture a second time. The facilitator asks participants to meditate on the word or phrase that speaks to them: "Let it interact with your thoughts, your hopes, your memories. Consider how the word or phrase is touching your life today."

The facilitator or other participant reads the scripture a third time saying, "Consider how God is calling you forth, inviting you, into doing or being through this reading. Allow God to use these words to touch you, shape you in life today."

Allow time for each person who would like to name the word or phrase, relevance or invitation.

AN ORDER FOR WEEKLY GATHERINGS

This order can be used each week. The scripture lesson and conversation starters are provided for each week.

Opening (3–5 minutes)
Participants greet one another as they find a seat.

Lighting the Candle
Light the candle as an invitation to the presence of God.

Prayer
O Holy Spirit, divine companion, we gather in response to your gracious invitation. We are here to listen, to wonder, and to learn. We are here to grow closer to one another and to you. Hear our prayers. Forgive our sins and heal our wounds. Raise us up so that we might be true disciples. In the name of Jesus our Savior, we pray. Amen.

Reading the Word (5 minutes) or *Lectio Divina* (30 minutes)
Ask a volunteer to read the scripture aloud one time. After a moment

of silence, the facilitator should read the scripture aloud a second time. Or use the guidelines for *lectio divina* on pages 78–79.

Reflecting on the Invitation (15 minutes)

Invite participants to sit in groups of two or three. Give them a few minutes to reflect on their *Wonderings* from the week's reading.

Which Wondering captured your imagination?

Which Wondering felt like an invitation? What kind of invitation was it—an invitation to do, to be, to leave behind?

How does the scripture lesson today clarify or deepen your thoughts from the week?

Responding to the Invitation (20 minutes)

Invite participants to engage in the described activity to delve deeper into the invitation for the week. Allow time for persons who feel comfortable to share briefly their responses to the invitation.

Closing (3–5 minutes)

The facilitator extinguishes the candle with words of encouragement.

Week One

Invitation to Life at Its Best

Opening (3–5 minutes)

Participants greet one another as they find a seat.

Lighting the Candle

Light the candle as an invitation to the presence of God.

Prayer

O Holy Spirit, divine companion, we gather in response to your gracious invitation. We are here to listen, to wonder, and to learn. We are here to grow closer to one another and to you. Hear our prayers. Forgive our sins and heal our wounds. Raise us up so that we might be true disciples. In the name of Jesus our Savior, we pray. Amen.

Reading the Word (5 minutes) or *Lectio Divina* (30 minutes)
John 10:10

"I came that they may have life, and have it abundantly."

Ask a volunteer to read the scripture aloud one time. After a moment of silence, the facilitator should read the scripture aloud a second time. Or use the guidelines for *lectio divina* on pages 78–79.

Reflecting on the Invitation (15 minutes)

Invite participants to sit in groups of two or three. Give them a couple minutes to reflect on their *Wonderings* from the week's reading.

Which Wondering captured your imagination?
Which Wondering felt like an invitation? What kind of
invitation was it—an invitation to do, to be, to leave behind?
How does the scripture lesson today clarify or deepen your
thoughts from the week?

Responding to the Invitation (20 minutes)
Explain that each person will have twenty minutes to write about the
invitations he or she has received. How are these invitations similar
to invitations Jesus offers in the Gospels; how do they differ? Ask
each person to write about what he or she hopes to learn in the
following five weeks of group study. What invitation is he or she
longing to hear from Jesus?

Closing (3–5 minutes)
Extinguish the candle saying, "May you choose to open, explore, and
respond to Jesus' invitation to you in the coming week."

Week Two

Invitation to Transforming Intimacy

Opening (3–5 minutes)

Participants greet one another as they find a seat.

Lighting the Candle

Light the candle as an invitation to the presence of God.

Prayer

O Holy Spirit, divine companion, we gather in response to your gracious invitation. We are here to listen, to wonder, and to learn. We are here to grow closer to one another and to you. Hear our prayers. Forgive our sins and heal our wounds. Raise us up so that we might be true disciples. In the name of Jesus our Savior, we pray. Amen.

Reading the Word (5 minutes) or *Lectio Divina* (30 minutes)
Matthew 22:34-40

When the Pharisees heard that he had silenced the Sadducees, they gathered together, and one of them, a lawyer, asked him a question to test him. "Teacher, which commandment in the law is the greatest?" He said to him, " 'You shall love the Lord your God with all your heart, and with all your soul, and with all your mind.' This is the greatest and first commandment. And a second is like it: 'You shall love your neighbor as yourself.' On these two commandments hang all the law and the prophets."

Ask a volunteer to read the scripture aloud one time. After a moment of silence, the facilitator should read the scripture aloud a second time. Or use the guidelines for *lectio divina* on pages 78–79.

Reflecting on the Invitation (15 minutes)

Invite participants to sit in groups of two or three. Give them a couple minutes to reflect on their *Wonderings* from the week's reading.

Which Wondering captured your imagination?

Which Wondering felt like an invitation? What kind of invitation was it—an invitation to do, to be, to leave behind?

How does the scripture lesson today clarify or deepen your thoughts from the week?

Responding to the Invitation (20 minutes)

Explain that each person will have ten to twelve minutes to respond in of these two ways—(1) experiment with a love word, repeating it over and over in silence and inviting God to reveal God's self in this time or (2) use the silence to confess where he or she has failed in loving others and feels God's response of grace and peace. Use either of these options as a way of inviting God's love to be made real.

Encourage persons to spread out in the room, to find a place that feels safe and comfortable. After ten to twelve minutes, invite persons back together.

Closing (3–5 minutes)

Extinguish the candle saying, "May we strive this week to love others and ourselves the way God loves us."

Week Three

Invitation to Transforming Discipleship

Opening (3–5 minutes)

Participants greet one another as they find a seat.

Lighting the Candle

Light the candle as an invitation to the presence of God.

Prayer

O Holy Spirit, divine companion, we gather in response to your gracious invitation. We are here to listen, to wonder, and to learn. We are here to grow closer to one another and to you. Hear our prayers. Forgive our sins and heal our wounds. Raise us up so that we might be true disciples. In the name of Jesus our Savior, we pray. Amen.

Reading the Word (5 minutes) or *Lectio Divina* (30 minutes)
Matthew 9:9-13

As Jesus was walking along, he saw a man called Matthew sitting at the tax booth; and he said to him, "Follow me." And he got up and followed him.

And as he sat at dinner in the house, many tax collectors and sinners came and were sitting with him and his disciples. When the Pharisees saw this, they said to his disciples, "Why does your teacher eat with tax collectors and sinners?" But when he heard this, he said, "Those who are well have no need of a physician, but those who are sick. Go and learn what this means, 'I desire mercy, not sacrifice.' For

I have come to call not the righteous but sinners."

Ask a volunteer to read the scripture aloud one time. After a moment of silence, the facilitator should read the scripture aloud a second time. Or use the guidelines for *lectio divina* on pages 78–79.

Reflecting on the Invitation (15 minutes)

Invite participants to sit in groups of two or three. Give them a couple minutes to reflect on their *Wonderings* from the week's reading.

Which Wondering captured your imagination?

Which Wondering felt like an invitation? What kind of invitation was it—an invitation to do, to be, to leave behind? How does the scripture lesson today clarify or deepen your thoughts from the week?

Responding to the Invitation (20 minutes)

Give the group members pen and paper (or have the participants open their journals to a blank page). Explain that they will have ten minutes to draw the story line of their lives. This may be a linear time line or a flow chart of arrows and loops and dead ends. It may be a physical map of a particular place where geography illustrates his or her story. Ask, "Where is the story going next?"

After ten minutes, ask each person to circle the times, places, or persons in his or her story when he or she needed to hear, "You are accepted." Then invite the participants into five minutes of silent prayer. Ask them to hear the whisper of Christ into the deepest places of their hearts and minds, "You are accepted."

Closing (3–5 minutes)

Extinguish the candle saying, "One of our deepest needs is for an experience of power from beyond ourselves that helps us become the people we long to be. May we receive Jesus' invitation to follow him knowing that we are accepted."

Week Four

Invitation to Transforming Solitude

Opening (3–5 minutes)

Participants greet one another as they find a seat.

Lighting the Candle

Light the candle as an invitation to the presence of God.

Prayer

O Holy Spirit, divine companion, we gather in response to your gracious invitation. We are here to listen, to wonder, and to learn. We are here to grow closer to one another and to you. Hear our prayers. Forgive our sins and heal our wounds. Raise us up so that we might be true disciples. In the name of Jesus our Savior, we pray. Amen.

Reading the Word (5 minutes) or *Lectio Divina* (30 minutes)
1 Kings 19:3-9

Then [Elijah] was afraid; he got up and fled for his life, and came to Beer-sheba, which belongs to Judah; he left his servant there.

But he himself went a day's journey into the wilderness, and came and sat down under a solitary broom tree. He asked that he might die: "It is enough; now, O LORD, take away my life, for I am no better than my ancestors." Then he lay down under the broom tree and fell asleep. Suddenly an angel touched him and said to him, "Get up and eat." He looked, and there at his head was a cake baked on hot stones, and a jar of water. He ate and drank, and lay down again. The angel of the LORD came a second time, touched him, and said, "Get up and eat, otherwise the journey will be too much for you." He got up, and ate and drank; then he went in the strength of that food forty days and forty nights to Horeb the mount of God. At that place he came to a cave, and spent the night there.

Then the word of the LORD came to him, saying, "What are you doing here, Elijah?"

Ask a volunteer to read the scripture aloud one time. After a moment of silence, the facilitator should read the scripture aloud a second time. Or use the guidelines for *lectio divina* on pages 78–79.

Reflecting on the Invitation (15 minutes)
Invite participants to sit in groups of two or three. Give them a couple minutes to reflect on their *Wonderings* from the week's reading.
Which Wondering captured your imagination?
Which Wondering felt like an invitation? What kind of invitation was it—an invitation to do, to be, to leave behind?
How does the scripture lesson today clarify or deepen your thoughts from the week?

Responding to the Invitation (20 minutes)
Explain to the participants that they will have a few minutes to imagine resting underneath their unique broom tree. Ask them to close their eyes to imagine where that place might be—in nature, a comfortable chair in their home, a sanctuary, or other place.

After a few moments ask the participants to spread out around the room and continue to imagine themselves under the broom tree. Allow them simply to rest in the solitude.

Closing (3–5 minutes)

Extinguish the candle saying, "We give thanks for these moments of silence. May we take the refreshment and calm with us into the week ahead."

WEEK FIVE

INVITATION TO TRANSFORMING MISSION

Opening (3–5 minutes)

Participants greet one another as they find a seat.

Lighting the Candle

Light the candle as an invitation to the presence of God.

Prayer

O Holy Spirit, divine companion, we gather in response to your gracious invitation. We are here to listen, to wonder, and to learn. We are here to grow closer to one another and to you. Hear our prayers. Forgive our sins and heal our wounds. Raise us up so that we might be true disciples. In the name of Jesus our Savior, we pray. Amen.

Reading the Word (5 minutes) or *Lectio Divina* (30 minutes)

Luke 11:1-4

[Jesus] was praying in a certain place, and after he had finished, one of his disciples said to him, "Lord, teach us to pray, as John taught his disciples." He said to them, "When you pray, say:
Father, hallowed be your name.

Your kingdom come.

Give us each day our daily bread.

And forgive us our sins,

for we ourselves forgive everyone indebted to us.

And do not bring us to the time of trial."

Ask a volunteer to read the scripture aloud one time. After a moment of silence, the facilitator should read the scripture aloud a second time. Or use the guidelines for *lectio divina* on pages 78–79.

Reflecting on the Invitation (15 minutes)

Invite participants to sit in groups of two or three. Give them a couple minutes to reflect on their *Wonderings* from the week's reading.

Which Wondering captured your imagination?

Which Wondering felt like an invitation? What kind of invitation was it—an invitation to do, to be, to leave behind? How does the scripture lesson today clarify or deepen your thoughts from the week?

Responding to the Invitation (20 minutes)

Our desire is to become like the God that we worship. Write the following sentences on a dry erase board or newsprint where everyone can see them.

I believe God is _____ and therefore God loves _____.

I believe God is _____ and therefore God acts _____.

I believe God is _____ and therefore God hates _____.

I believe God is _____ and therefore God sees _____.

I believe God is _____ and therefore God wants _____.

I believe God is _____ and therefore God needs _____.

Ask participants to write and finish these sentences in their journals. They may want to add their own sentences. Then ask participants to imagine God inviting them into mission in the world. What does it look like? Where is it? Who might they walk alongside of, stand against, or love that surprises them? Invite them to write about this invitation and call to mission.

Finally, ask participants to join together in groups of two or three. Trevor says that we may need to revise our image of God. Talk together about how this week's reading and reflection enhance or even change their image of God.

Closing (3–5 minutes)

Extinguish the candle and invite the participants to join you in the Lord's Prayer. Ask each member to focus on the *us* and *our* while reciting the prayer.

WEEK SIX

INVITATION TO TRANSFORMING MYSTERY

Opening (3–5 minutes)
Participants greet one another as they find a seat.

Lighting the Candle
Light the candle as an invitation to the presence of God.

Prayer
O Holy Spirit, divine companion, we gather in response to your gracious invitation. We are here to listen, to wonder, and to learn. We are here to grow closer to one another and to you. Hear our prayers. Forgive our sins and heal our wounds. Raise us up so that we might be true disciples. In the name of Jesus our Savior, we pray. Amen.

Reading the Word (5 minutes) or *Lectio Divina* (30 minutes)
John 12:20-26
Now among those who went up to worship at the festival were some Greeks. They came to Philip, who was from Bethsaida in Galilee, and said to him, "Sir, we wish to see Jesus." Philip went and told Andrew; then Andrew and Philip went and told Jesus. Jesus answered them, "The hour has come for the Son of Man to be glorified. Very truly, I tell you, unless a grain of wheat falls into the earth and dies, it remains just a single grain; but if it dies, it bears much fruit. Those who love their life lose it, and those who hate their life in this world will keep it for eternal life. Whoever serves me must follow me, and where I

am, there will my servant be also. Whoever serves me, the Father will honor.

Ask a volunteer to read the scripture aloud one time. After a moment of silence, the facilitator should read the scripture aloud a second time. Or use the guidelines for *lectio divina* on pages 78–79.

Reflecting on the Invitation (15 minutes)

Invite participants to sit in groups of two or three. Give them a couple minutes to reflect on their *Wonderings* from the week's reading.

Which Wondering captured your imagination?

Which Wondering felt like an invitation? What kind of invitation was it—an invitation to do, to be, to leave behind?

How does the scripture lesson today clarify or deepen your thoughts from the week?

Responding to the Invitation (20 minutes)

Ask each participant to imagine the loss or death that he or she is living now. Invite each person to close his or her fist tightly around that loss. Imagine it as a seed buried deep in the earth. Ask God to let the Holy Spirit rain down the water of desire, water of hope, and water of transformation that will allow you to open your hand and let the new thing blossom.

As they are ready, invite the participants to open their hands and imagine this new mystery unfolding in their lives.

Closing (3–5 minutes)

Extinguish the candle saying, "We remember that to hold on to life is to lose it. Go now with confidence that to lose life is to find it."